Python

The Ultimate Beginner's Guide for Becoming Fluent in Python Programming

Mark Chen

Table of Content

Introduction

The Python Programming language stands alongside the top-rated and most widely used programming languages out there due to its simplicity and versatility. That makes it a very easy language to pick up and implement into the real world to digitally carve out solutions to real life issues. If you are eagerly chomping at the bit to jump into the world of programming, then this is what you will want to learn! And the best part of Python is that applications written by this particular language are often five times shorter than Java and almost ten times shorter than C++!

There are some people who prefer to learn a new programming language as a hobby, but then there are those who aim to pursue it to build a career upon it. If you are one of the latter, then we are happy to tell you that the level of job opportunity for Python has been constantly on the rise since 2013 with an average of 19% per year. If this rising trend continues, then by the time you have mastered this language, job companies will run after you instead of the other way around!

With a programming language like Python in your skill set, you will not only become a more attractive option for employers, but this will further encourage you to work on pet projects by yourself as well!

If you lean more towards the side of web development instead of application creation, then you should know that world famous social networking websites such as Pinterest and Instagram are made up of an open source web application that goes by the name of Django. And guess what? The overall frameworks of these websites are created by none other than Python, using the software mentioned. Django only provides the platform, but the whole backdrop of a great looking site such as Instagram is created through Python.

If you feel like you have the courage and tenacity to continue down this path and carry out the journey until the end, then we welcome you into the world of Python Programming.

Let Us Begin....

Chapter One: Getting to Know Your Python

We do realize that the title might be a little bit misleading, and no, we are not going to be talking about how to identify your pet snake. (Kudos to you if you have one!) Instead, we are going to hold your hand, take you along for a brief walk, and let you slowly dive into the world of Python programming!

What Exactly is Python?

Python is widely regarded as being the "Right Tool for the Job" thanks to its extremely versatile capabilities, which makes it on par with any of the high-level programming languages out there. The language can also be extended and/or embedded as a tool for writing macros. The flexibility of Python ultimately makes it a great option for solving both high and low level programs, but due to some of its minor drawbacks, the prowess of this language drops down a bit when trying to deal with some specific computing tasks.

Let us individually tackle the various aspects of Python now:

Why Python is Awesome

The emergence of this language took place during the 1980s. At that time, there were several programming languages out there, but none had the flexibility or versatility which the creator of Python, Guido Van Rossum, required. Throughout his quest, he was finally able to develop Python, which had the following dream features:

- **The Ability to Act as a Scripting Language:** Keep in mind that a "script" is essentially a program which gives you the ability to control other programs. Kind of like a human mind control device, but for the computer! Scripting languages during that time slowly rose into the limelight, thanks to their efficiency in allowing a user to develop prototypes and pass messages from one component to the next. The scripting aspect of Python has evolved beyond that and is much more powerful, so that now the whole Python language is referred to as a "Dynamic Programming Language."

- **The Father Of Statement Grouping:** If you are at least a little bit familiar with programming, then you should know that languages such as Java or C++ uses a { to begin a block of code and ends them with }, enclosing the statements in individual blocks, making it easy to debug, leading to fewer errors. Apparently Python was the language which brought this practice into the limelight, and it was the first of its kind to enforce indentation of code blocks.

- **High Level Data Compatibility:** We all know that computers only understand the digital language of 0 and 1. But is that suitable for humans? Not necessarily! Human beings are accustomed to a more complex form of text, which in the programming world is known as "high-level data." Python is a language which makes it much easier for the manipulation of these high-level data, thanks to the myriad of manipulating options that it offers, including the slicing, joining or splitting of strings.

- **The Power to Utilize Plugins and Extensions:** In modern day programming, the ability to be able to extend a language is very important, as it allows a bunch of new features to be added. This makes the language much more compatible with newer data types, applications and operating systems. Thankfully, Python has a very large library of modules and plug-ins coming in from both its core developers and the community at large, constantly evolving the language and pushing its potential forward.

- **A Form of Interpreted Language:** It should be kept in mind that an interpreted language is essentially a language that can be run directly off the human-written source code. (An alternative like C++ has to convert the written code into Machine Language before being able to run.) This ability of Python allows debugging to occur much more quickly, as the programmer is able to directly identify his/her mistakes while writing the code on the fly.

- **The Built-In Text Manipulation System:** Unlike many programming languages out there, Python comes packed with a very strong integrated text manipulation and search feature, which allows the users to handle text sensitive/ heavy applications with much ease.

- **No Compile-Time Checking:** Having a Compile-Time checking system might be largely troublesome, as it might restrict the user from being allowed to test multiple modules at once. With the exclusion of that feature, Python supports the combination of multiple modules by bundling them into small packages, after which each module is allowed to be built and checked individually.

The Multiple Types of Programming Styles

Python is often regarded as a multi-paradigm programming language, which basically means that it is comprised of multiple programming philosophies packed in one language.

- **OOP:** Object Oriented Programming (OOP) has been gaining mass popularity these days for its ability to break down larges codes into tiny bits for easier passing. Python is fully compatible with this practice.

- **The Best of Other Worlds:** The versatility of Python has led to its adopting some of the core features of other widely used languages. So, if you have ever worked on any of the following, then you will feel right at home with Python.

    o **Java:** Python takes the OOP aspect from this guy.

    o **Perl:** The framework of Perl is responsible for giving Python the ability to deeply manipulate texts and encourage web development.

    o **Tel:** This contributes to Python's scripting and GUI developing capabilities.

o **Scheme:** This is responsible for teaching Python how to perform complex calculations by using functions.

Chapter One: Study Questions

Q1) What is Python?

a) A procedural programming language that can be extended to be used as tool for Javascript.

b) A procedural programming language that cannot be extended to be used as tool for macros.

c) A non-procedural programming language that can be extended to be used as tool for macros.

d) A procedural programming language that can be extended to be used as tool for macros.

Answer: D

Q2) Who is regarded as the creator of Python

a) Guido Van Rossum

b) Lidvan Van Dutch

c) Iguana De Fox

d) Vincent Gale

Answer: A

Q3) What is a script?

a) It is essentially a method to call upon other functions

b) It is a way of communicating with different parts of the same program

c) It is essentially a program that gives you the ability to control other programs

d) All of the above

Answer: C

Q4) What is statement grouping?

a) It allows the program to separate different chunks of code

b) It allows the program to join all the different parts of the code

c) It allows different parts of the code to be deleted easily

d) It is a way to send parameters to different functions

Answer: A

Q5) Python has the components of which of these languages?

a) Java

b) Perl

c) Tel

d) All of the above

Answer: D

Chapter Two: The Various Components of Python Programming

Now that we have discussed the very essence of Python programming, let's not waste any more time, and jump into the technical aspects of Python programming right away!

The Cooking Analogy When Writing Programs

Before even beginning to build up a building, an architect is hired to carve out the blueprint of the building upon which the whole structure will be built. Later on that same blueprint can be utilized as a reference for creating other buildings as well.

When programming with Python or any other language, it is essential to keep the following things in mind before even touching the keyboard:

- Fully understand the problem you want to solve.
- Discuss and think about the possible solutions to that problem.

- Establish a pseudo code/ flowchart in order to clearly draw out the steps which you are going to follow in order to achieve your solution.
- Convert your pseudocode into the respective programming language.

Keep in mind, though, that in terms of programming, there are various similar components that are commonly found in multiple programs. So it is always wise to keep your solved problems at hand, because you might want to have it as a reference when trying to solve another similar problem.

The Ways of Dealing with Python

The flexibility of Python has given it a very nice and accessible system, which opens up the gateways for absolutely new programmers, as well as advanced developers. At its core, Python has two different modes through which you can approach this language.

- Interactive
- IDLE Musing

Interactive Mode

The first mode that we will be discussing here is the Interactive mode, which is dedicated to first-time programmers and/or beginner programs. This mode allows the user to send Python one instruction at a time or write small pieces to instantly analyze how Python handles them. The procedure through which Python deals with the input lines is similar to how the operating system (Shell) utilizes simple commands such as mouse click.

The interactive mode is designed in such a manner that it gives you a great deal of freedom when working with text manipulation, modules, functions or even small parts of large programs to verify and test out their integrity.

Given the openness of Python's interactive mode, we would like to consider this mode as being:

- A sandbox to experiment with whatever Python has to offer
- A guide through which you will be able to learn more about Python
- A convenient and reliable tool to smash out the bugs in your written programs

How to Start the Interactive Mode

Firing up the Interactive mode is pretty easy, just follow these simple steps.

- Open up your command console. Depending on your OS, the procedure might vary a little.
- For Mac OS, you will need to open up your Terminal Application and Select File- New Shell
- In Windows, you will need to open up your Command Prompt Window
- For UNIX you will need to type Python in your existing shell windows.

Type python. That's it! Once done, you should have something that looks like the picture below.

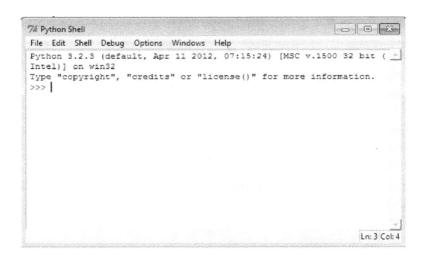

The Traditional First Program: "Hello World"

From one program to the next, it has been hailed as a tradition of starting the journey by typing in the Hello World program.

This is primarily done because in any language, Hello World is the most simplistic and shortest program to run.

While in Java the Hello World program spans for about 5 lines, in Python it runs just 1 line.

Now, before we tell you to write down the program, you should be aware of the rules of engagement as followed in the interactive mode for Python. This simply explains the basic methodology of how the interactive mode works and is comprised of just two steps:

- Type your desired statement or expression
- Press the Enter key for your result

These two instructions are at the heart of the interactive mode, and are followed when writing any program in interactive mode.

For the Hello World program, we are going to be typing the following statement. Behold your first program!

```
>>> print "Hello, World!"
Hello, World!
```

So far so good! See, this is the magic of interactive mode. You will always get your results in an instant.

Let's explore this even further.

While in the interactive mode, if you want the program to return the information of any store object, then the steps are:

- Type the name of the object and press Enter
- Alternatively, you can use the print command and the name of the object as well

So far so good! See, this is the magic of interactive mode. You will always get your results in an instant.

Let's explore this even further.

While in the interactive mode, if you want the program to return the information of any store object, then the steps are:

- Type the name of the object and press Enter
- Alternatively, you can use the print command and the name of the object as well

Integers

When dealing with integers, the action performed is similar to the example below.

```
>>> x = [3,2]
>>> x
 [3, 2]
>>> print x
 [3, 2]
```

Strings

However, when working with strings, there's a slight difference which you should keep in mind. Observe the example below:

```
>>> x = "mystring"
>>> x
"mystring"
>>> print x
mystring
```

Notice that when you are typing just the name of the object containing the string, the result comes with the quotation marks. Alternatively, when using the command "print," the quotation marks are gone.

To understand the why this difference occurs, you should realize that pressing the enter button alone (without the print command) acts as an internal command which calls the repr() function, while using "print" calls the function str().

The repr() function is designed to return the value in the canonical form, while str() returns it in "nice" form. Below is an example to further clarify the difference between these two.

```
>>> 3.2 # canonical
3.2000000000000002
>>>str(3.2) # nice
'3. 2'
>>>repr(3.2) # canonical
'3.2000000000000002'
>>> print 3.2 # nice
3.2
```

Code Block

When calling the name of a Code Block, for example a class instance or a function, the program will be retuning you the storage location and/or name, data type of the said Code Block.

```
>>> class Message:
...         pass
...
>>>str(Message)
'__main__.Message'
>>>repr(Message)
'<class __main__.Message at
0x58e40>'
```

The Secret Storage Unit

Whenever you are working with Python, you should bear in mind that he immediate last printed result is always stored in a secret container which has a special name: the underscore character. This feature is only available in the interactive mode.

```
>>> "Hello, World!"
'Hello, World!'
>>> _
'Hello, World!'
```

Please take note that this does not work on assignment statements or print commands. It only holds the value of the preceding expression.

```
>>> "Hello, Nurse!"
'Hello, Nurse!'
>>> x = 35
>>> _
'Hello, Nurse!'
```

Interactive Mode as a Simple Calculator

Here is an example of how you can take advantage of the interactive mode's capability for manipulating numbers to perform simple calculation. As you can see, after typing the expression, pressing the Enter key will return the result of the calculation.

```
>>> (1 + 3) * (2 + 2)
16
>>> 1 + 3 * 2 + 2
9
```

You can use the variable as well to perform more delicate calculations.

```
>>> x = 1 + 3
>>> y = 2 + 2
>>> x * y
16
```

29

Understanding The Mathematics Module

Aside from the common arithmetic operators (+ and -), Python also gives you access to a wide range of mathematical functions thanks to the integrated math module. An example is given below, and more regarding this chapter is discussed later on.

Round()

The round function acts as an interpolation device, which takes a floating number as input and rounds it up to the nearest whole number before sending the result.

```
>>> round(9.9)
10.0
>>> round(9.3)
9.0
```

Reminding Yourself of Your Variables

If you are planning to write a long program, then there may be some time when you will need to recall the names of the variables which you have initialized and maybe take note of them. To create a list of all the names of objects, modules and functions used in a specific namespace (particular part of the program) you will need to use the dir () function.

```
% python
Python 2.5b1 (r25b1:47038M, Jun 20
2006, 16:17:55)

>>>dir()
['__builtins__', '__doc__',
'___name___']
>>>too_many_cats = "Impossible!"
>>>dir()
['__builtins__', '__doc__',
'___name___', 'too___many___cats']
```

Initiating Multiline Programs in Interactive Mode

So far we have dealt with small programs that are comprised of only one line. But what if you wanted to go beyond that and create multiline programs? Well, lucky for you, the interactive mode allows you to do that as well.

But before doing so, keep in mind that there is no built-in saving mechanism for Python's interactive mode, so it is wise to keep your code saved in a separate text file for future reference.

As an example, here is a very simple program which converts kilometers to miles and vice versa. (Don't be alarmed if you don't understand the format; this is further discussed in later chapters.)

The Implementation of Scripts and Modules

Since the interactive mode of Python doesn't really allow you to save your codes when you quit, you are forced to store in them text files. Now, these specific text files containing Python codes are known as scripts or modules (depending on the length of code stored). Modules are tiny chunks of code and scripts are whole programs.

Running a Script

While working within the interactive mode, the Terminal program of Shell works similarly to a command prompt window. As such, a script can be run by typing in the following:

```
% python script.py
```

Note the text "script.py". The .py here is basically the extension through which Python understands that you are trying to run a script, and "script" is the name of your file name of your script.

Understand the skeleton; you should now be able to create your own script following the steps below.

- Let's say that you are typing these into your text editor:

```
print "testing how scripts and
interactive mode communicate"
x = 500
print "The value of x is ", x
```

- The next step is to save your file, keeping in mind that .py is the extension here. So your file can be newscript.py

Finally, to run the script enter the following code:

```
% python -i tinyscript.py
testing how scripts and interactive
mode communicate
The value of x is 500
>>>
```

- Keep in mind that the python – simply means that the script that you are loading is to run in command interactive mode.

How to Import a Module in Interactive Mode

As mentioned earlier, modules are chunks of code which can be imported into the interactive mode interface allowing, them to be used in conjunction with a larger program. When imported, Python runs the code encapsulated within the module and stores it in the namespace.

Let take an example where we have a module called tinymodule.py that includes the following function:

```
>>> import tinymodule
```

The important thing to keep in mind here is that to import a module, you will need to exclude the .py extension.

Once imported, if you then want to access an attribute of the module, you will need to do it as follows.

Continuing from our tinymodule example:

```
>>> x = tinymodule.tinyfunction(2)
testing how modules and interactive
```

```
mode communicate
you passed me the parameter 2
2 squared is 4
```

The Concept of IDLE Musing

Now that we have discussed the interactive mode, it's time to talk a little bit about the Interactive Development Environment or IDLE for short. This is an editing program that has been entirely designed via Python by the famed Guido Van Rossum himself! Whenever you are installing any newer version of Python on your computer, IDLE is automatically installed, so there's no need to browse around for any extra software.

Firing Up the IDLE

Once you have clicked on the button to open up your IDLE, you will be greeted with a similar window as shown below. You mightsee a number of other windows as well, but you can safely ignore them for now.

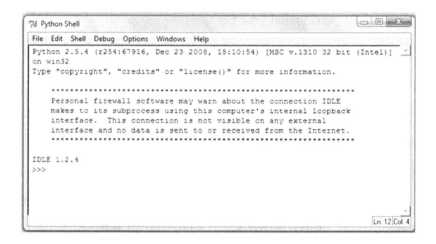

The Python Shell itself runs in interactive mode, and so displays the similar Python prompt, >>>

Writing Up Your First Statement and Program Inside the Python Shell

Working in the IDLE Python Shell is very similar to working in the interactive mode, with just a few minor differences:

- Here when you are writing code, various parts are colorized accordingly, making it much easier for you to identify different parts of your code.
- When dealing with multiline statements, IDLE prevents it from showing the continuation prompt.
- You don't have to worry about indents here as they are automatically given by the shell itself.

An example of the Hello World program which we wrote earlier in Python Shell would be:

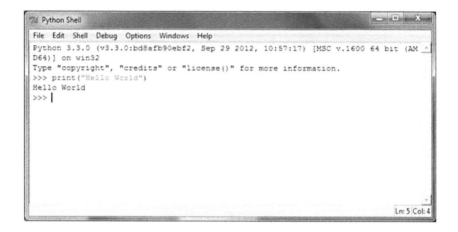

Let's Meet the IDLE's Internal Text Editor

IDLE comes freshly built with an internal text editor, which allows you to modify or create your very own modules and scripts. Unlike the integrated mode's file opening system, the IDLE's is pretty straight forward.

- For opening up a new text editing screen, simply click on the File
- To open up an existing module or script, click on the File button, then the Open button, and browse to your designated file.

Similarly, if you want to run a script or module, keep in mind that the code should be open in the text editor. While open, click on the Run button and click Run Module

Chapter Two: Study Questions

Q1) Which of the following is a good practice for writing programs?

a) It is essential to go head first into the problem without prior thinking.

b) It is not recommended to discuss the whole problem with someone before moving forward

c) It is recommended to establish a pseudo code

d) One should not convert the pseudo- code into the respective programming language

Answer: B

Q2) Which one of the following is a way interact with Python?

a) IDLE Musing

b) Command Line Interpretation

c) Kernel Manipulation

d) Through a notepad

Answer: A

Q3) Which one of the following programming mode is dedicated towards beginners?

a) Functional programming

b) Modular programming

c) Interactive programming mode

d) Object Oriented Mode

Answer: C

Q4) Which of the following code will run a Hello World program?

a) >>> show "Hello, World!"

Hello, World!

b) >>> post "Hello, World!"

Hello, World!

c) >>> generate "Hello, World!"

Hello, World!

d) >>> print "Hello, World!"

Hello, World!

Answer: D

Q5) Using the round() method to 9.9, what will be the answer?

a) 9.5

b) 10

c) 11

d) 9

Answer: B

Chapter Three: Beginning Your Journey as Programmer

Now that you have a basic grasp of the whole Python programming scene, it's time to actually learn what the fundamental building blocks of Python are and how you can manipulate them in order to create your own program. Up until now we introduced you to some very basic and stock programs. The concepts from here on out are going to help you carve out the solution to any and every problem that you might face, with just a bit of wit!

But before diving headfirst into the syntaxes, you must first learn some of the good practices that every budding programmer should follow.

The Must Be Followed Rules (The Three D's)

The following rules should be kept in mind whenever working with a larger program, otherwise you leave yourself open to the risk of being hammered by other programmers!

- **Documentation:** Documentation is the process of making sure that your program and your source code are written in as simplistic a manner as possible, so that another programmer is able to look at it and understand what you are trying to deliver right away.

- **Efficient Designing:** This is strictly important and should be kept in mind. Anyone can build a program that can get the job done, but being able to design a program that is carefully molded to be able to tackle any problem effectively and efficiently is a skill that will separate you from an amateur programmer.

- **Debugging:** This is essentially the process of making sure that your program is free from any glaring errors.

Maintaining Your Program

So, you have finally completed your first program. Is that the end of the journey for you? Probably not, because in this gradually evolving world, you are going to need to perhaps add new features or change the existing ones to keep up with everything.

For example, let's assume that you have created a program which is designed to send the first ten lines from your calendar file. Let's call it daily_calender.py

```
importsmtplib # get the module for
sending email
```

```
my_address = 'me@example.com'
headers = [ 'Subject: Daily
calendar',
'From: ' + my_address,
'To: ' + my_address,
] # this list spans four lines for
readability
entries = open('my_calendar').
msg = '\r\n'.join(headers) + '\r\n'
+ ''.join(entries)
smtp = smtplib.SMTP('mail') #
replace 'mail' with the name of your
mailhost
smtp.sendmail(my_address,
[my_address], msg)
smtp.close()
```

After a few weeks, you now change your mind and decide that you want your program to send you a large update once a week instead of sending an update every single day. So, you copy the lines from the previous program and simply add newer lines incorporating the if and else statements which we will discuss later.

```
importsmtplib, sys
my_address = 'me@example.com'
```

```python
if sys.argv[1] == 'weekly':
headers = [ 'Subject: Weekly
calendar',
'From: ' + my_address,
'To: ' + my_address,
]
entries = open('my_calendar').
msg = '\r\n'.join(headers) + ''.join
(entries)
smtp = smtplib.SMTP('mail')
smtp.sendmail(my_address,
[my_address], msg)
smtp.close()
else:
headers = [ 'Subject: Daily
calendar',
'From: ' + my_address,
'To: ' + my_address,
]
entries =
open('my_calendar').readlines()[:10]
msg = '\r\n'.join(headers) +
''.join(entries)
smtp = smtplib.SMTP('mail')
smtp.sendmail(my_address,
[my_address], msg)
smtp.close()
```

This process of upgrading your code in such a way so that it avoids repetition by taking the already repeated codes and turn them into chunks, available for another program, is known as program refactoring.

Naming Conventions to Keep in Mind

These are like grammar for the programming world. If you are able to have a good grasp of them, then your programs will be much less prone to being affected by any kind of error.

- Always make sure to keep variable names as easy and simple as possible. For example, if you want to create a code which is designed to extract a zip code from a customer database, you might go for:

```
customer_zip = get_zip(Pandora)
```

- Make sure to name your modules or packages using lowercase, keeping the length short.

```
likethis
```

- Make sure to start the name of classes with a capital letter embedded capitals.

```
LikeThis
```

- Make sure to end the names of error-type exceptions using Error

Always name functions and methods using lowercase characters. Underscores are allowed here.

```
like_this
```

- Again when declaring constants, you should always use all capital letters.

```
LIKETHIS
```

- Make sure to remember that names are case sensitive, so NUM will be read as a different element from nUm.

- Make sure to always start a name with a letter or underscore.

Programming Format

The following are some guidelines which you should keep in mind in order to make sure that your code is much more readable.

- Make sure to indent each block of code by four spaces
- If you have a long line, make sure to use (), {} or []
- Alternatively, strings should be continued using / which can also be used for making comments to let other programmers know what you were trying to achieve.

```
parrot = "This parrot is no more! He
has ceased to
be! He's expired \
o and gone to meet his maker!
```

- Make sure to put spaces after and before using a = sign.

With the basic practices out of the way, let's now start talking about the individual moving parts of Python.

How a Value Is Stored

In every programming language there is a language to assign values to different variables (containers). In Python the rule is very simple:

```
num = 45
```

The above statement indicates that the value 45 is stored in the variable named num.

Always remember that the string/number to the right side of the "=" sign gets assigned to the variable at the left side, which can then be called upon later in the program.

```
mynewname = "myvalue"
mynewname = myname
```

The Difference Between Statements and Expressions

Up until now you have already seen us use terms like literals, expressions and statements. Let us break these down for you now. While understanding these is not strictly essential to programming, it's still a smart move to know about them.

- **Literal:** This is basically a word or a chunk of text in Python which acts as a container holding a certain value. When running a program, Python automatically creates objects bases on the specified literals.

- **Statement:** A statement is essentially a command that tells Python what it should do. For example, when you are assigning a value to the variable x, as x = 35, it is a statement. Again, when you are writing print x, that is also a statement telling Python to print the value of x.

- **Expression:** The sentences that perform one or more operations to produce a result are known as expressions. Such operations can include the involvement of literals, functions or even method calls.

Have a look at the example below, which should give you a clear idea about expression and statement.

```
>>> "monty python" # This is an
expression and a
literal.
'monty python'
>>> x = 25 # This is a statement. 25
is a
literal.
>>>x# This is an expression.
25
>>> 2 in [1, 2, 3] # This is also an
expression.
True
>>>deffoo(): # This is a statement.
... return 1 # return is a
statement; 1 is an
expression.
```

```
...
>>>foo() # foo is a name; foo() is
an
expression.
1
```

The Importance of Data Types

When programming, you will usually need to pass information to your program in the form of data. Now, data in programs vary from one type to another, and depending on what you wish to do, you will have to choose the appropriate data type.

Let's have a look at the different data types of Python. Please note that here we are leaving out Sequences and Strings as we will be discussing those in detail later on.

- **Numbers:** These are simple data that have to do with numerical values when performing mathematical operations.

Type (keyword)	Example	Used for...
Plain integers (`int`) and long integers (`long`)	7 6666666666L	Whole numbers (long integers are very large whole numbers.)
Floating point numbers (`float`)	1.1714285714285713	Real numbers
Complex numbers (`complex`)	(3+4j)	Imaginary numbers
Decimal numbers (`decimal.Decimal`)	decimal.Decimal("181.2")	Calculations requiring decimal arithmetic

- **Sets:** Sets are similar to arrays in the sense that they have the capacity to hold multiple items, which can be of different types. It should be kept in mind, though, that each item in the set must be unique as well. The syntax for this one follows the word <u>set</u> by the name of the group of elements in brackets.

```
>>>mylist = ['spam', 'lovely',
'spam', 'glorious', 'spam']
>>> set(mylist)
set(['lovely', 'glorious', 'spam']
```

- **Files:** The File data type is used by Python whenever it has to deal with files present on the web or on your PC. Bear in mind that these are not the actual files, but just a mirror internal representation of the file themselves.

A simple example below opens up a file named myfile.

51

```
open("myfile")
```

A Little Insight into Operators

Operators are yet another set of tools that are used to manipulate data and information inside the Python framework. You may have seen simple mathematical operators such as + or − while using a calculator. Python incorporates all of those and much more; using these, you will be even able to manipulate strings. Operators in Python have been divided into 4 categories:

- Arithmetic
- Comparison
- Logical Boolean
- Conditional

We will be talking about the Arithmetic operator in great depth in the coming chapters, here we will discuss a bit about the last three.

The Comparison Operators

The comparison operators are often used when a comparison is needed to be made between two or more data. Based on the result, which is either TRUE or FALSE, the final output is made.

- Less Than (<)
- Greater Than (>)
- Equal To (==)
- Not Equal to (!= ; <>)

You already know about the comparison of simple numbers. Python also allows you to compare the level of strings as well. Have a look at the example below:

```
>>> 'a' < 'b'
            True


>>> 'z' < 'a'
            True
```

The War Between Yes or No! Boolean Operators

These are also referred to as being logical operators in the sense that they test the validity of any given expression and return the result as being either true or false. The internal mechanism is as follows:

- When using "and" the testing stops when a false condition is encountered
- Similarly, when "or" is used, the testing stops when a true condition is encountered

```
>>> '1' and 1 and 'one'
'one'
>>> '1' or 1 or 'one'
'1'
>>> (2 < 3) or (5 > 6)
True
```

Keep in mind that Python tests the expression from left to right and then returns the final value that is tested.

Chapter Three: Study Questions

Q1) Which one of the following is considered as one of the three D's of programming
a) Inefficient Designing
b) Defragmenting
c) Debugging
d) None of the above
Answer: D

Q2) Which one of the following is a process by which errors in a program can be eliminated
a) Documentation
b) Efficient Designing
c) Debugging
d) Defragmenting
Answer: D

Q3) Which of the following refers to the process of making sure that the source code is written in a simplistic manner?
a) Documentation
b) Efficient Designing
c) Debugging
d) Defragmentation
Answer: A

Q4) Which of the following is a wrong convention when writing class names?

a) LikeThis

b) Likethis

c) LIKETHIS

d) likeThis

Answer: A

Q5) How can you store a value?

a) num == 45

b) num =/ 30

c) num = 12

d) num =! 10

Answer: C

Chapter Four: How to Deal with Strings

Similar to most of the computer programming languages out there, a string typically consists of a number of text characters. It may be just a single character, multiple lines or a whole novella! This chapter is going to be dedicated to teaching you how manipulation of strings works in Python.

Let's start by explaining the differences between the numbers of quotation marks used. These are primarily focused on judging how your string is going to be formatted.

Single/Double Quotes

When creating strings in Python, you can either use a pair of single quote marks or double quote marks. Both of these essentially tell Python that you have a string encapsulated inside them.

```
>>> penguin = "on top of the
television set"
>>>what_it_is_doing =
```

Triple Quotes

Triple Quotes is a special case of quoting. When you use triple quotes in defining a string, when printed, the program is going to be printing your text in exactly the format you have written. So:

```
>>> spam = """
...               spam spamspamspamspam
...               and spam
... """
>>> print spam
spamspamspamspamspam
               and spam
```

Escape Characters

You are definitely not going to allow your characters to escape from your program, mind you! The Escape characters defined below are basically used to give the preceding character a special property. You always start a command with a backslash (\ ).

Let's have a look at the example below. In this scenario, looking at the sentence below, you want to quote between e and s of Where's to act as a generic character instead of a quote mark. The code will be as follows:

```
>>>whiteRabbit = 'Where\'s my
pocket-watch?'
>>> print whiteRabbit
Where's my pocket-watch?
```

Below is a list of all the escape characters which you will have control over in Python:

Character	Meaning
\ as last character on a line	Text on the next line goes with the text on this line.
\\	Backslash
\'	Single quote
\"	Double quote
\e	Escape key
\n	Linefeed
\t	Tab
\0 *nn*	Octal character (*nn* is a two-digit number)
\x *nn*	Hexadecimal character (*nn* is a two-digit number)

Alternatively, if you want a string to not look for any escape codes, then you can define the string as a raw string. This is done by adding the letter r before your first quotation mark.

```
>>> path = r"C:\Applications"
>>> print path
C:\Applications
```

Manipulating Multi Lined Strings

There are multiple ways in Python in which you will be able to write multi-lined sentences.

- Using the triple quotation method described earlier
- Using the linefeed escape code (\n) as such

```
>>> cheese = "cheeses
available:\nsavoyard\nboursin"
>>> print cheese
 cheeses available:
savoyard
boursin
```

- Again, if you want to combine two individual lines into a single string, you can do that through the following code:

```
>>> x = ("hello"
    ... "world")
>>> print x
helloworld
```

Unlocking The Anatomy of a String

Python has a very interesting way through which you will be able to actually observe how Python internally represents a string. All you have to do here is type the name of the string and press Enter.

Here, it is seen that Python represents a new line with the escape code of
\n:

```
>>>modernlife = "as i was surfing on
the air\n\
... i saw a spam that wasn't
>>>modernlife
"as i was surfing on the air\ni saw
a spam that
```

String Operators

Similar to operators that are involved when dealing with arithmetic entities, Python has a set of operators that are used when dealing with strings.

Concatenation (+)

These operators are basically used when you need to two separate strings to be joined together.

```
>>> toaster1 = "would you like some
toast? "
```

```
>>> toaster2 = "or how about
muffins??? \n"
>>>annoying_toaster = (toaster1 +
toaster2)* 3
>>> print annoying_toaster
would you like some toast? or how
about muffins???
would you like some toast? or how
about muffins???
would you like some toast? or how
about muffins???
```

The above example also shows the operation of the * operator
which repeats the printed line to the specified number.

The String Comparator

Just as in arithmetic you were able to compare the size of two
or more numerical values, the string operator allows you to
compare the size of strings using the < or > operator.

An example was already given in one of the prior chapters. We
will be using that example once again. Keeping in mind the
following points will help you a lot to understand the basis of
these comparisons.

- Beginning letters are smaller than ending letters, meaning a will be smaller than z.
- Capital letters are always considered as smaller than lowercase letters. So Y and Z are smaller than a.
- Digits are always smaller than letters, so 5 is smaller than A.
- Punctuation marks are considered as smaller than letters or numbers: ! is smaller than 5. However, there are some exceptions, such as ({}), (|) and (~) that are considered to be larger than the letters.

```
>>> 'A' < 'Z'
True
>>> 'b' > 'a'
True
>>> 'a' > 'z'
True
```

Introduction to String Methods

String methods are pre-determined sets of instructions embedded into the Python framework that will allow you to perform certain actions on your strings. To call upon a method, all you will have to do is write the name of the string, use dot and write the method name.

Count

For example, the following example counts the number of the letter "s" present in the string.

```
>>>mystring = "mississippi"
>>>mystring.count('s')
4
```

Content Check

This method will allow you to check whether or not your string has specific content, and the result will be returned as either true or false.

```
>>>mystring = 'the quick brown fox'
>>> 'goose' in mystring
False
```

Check The End Content

To check to see if a string ends with any specified content, you will need to use the following method:endswith. To begin, you go with the startswith method.

```
>>>mystring = 'the quick brown fox'
>>> 'goose' in mystring
False
```

```
>>>mystring.endswith('fox')
True
```

Sort Your Data

To sort the contents of a string, you can use the sort() method.

```
>>>mylist = ['whiskey', 'tango',
'foxtrot']
>>>mylist.sort()
>>>mylist
['foxtrot', 'tango', 'whiskey']
```

The sorting here is done based on the information which we described earlier regarding the priority of capital letters and lowercase letters.

Data Conversion to String

It is possible to convert any type of data to string using the built-in function of str()

```
>>>str(2345)
'2345'
```

Introduction to the Concept of Indexing and Slicing

		[6:10]									
0	1	2	3	4	5	6	7	8	9	10	11
M	o	n	t	y		P	y	t	h	o	n
−12	−11	−10	−9	−8	−7	−6	−5	−4	−3	−2	−1

[−12:−7]

In many programming languages and in Python, the data and information that you input are often separated into individual blocks called elements and are stored in a specific location called an index. Each index contains one element from the data at hand. In terms of strings, when talking about indexing, we are essentially breaking down the whole string and considering each character as being a single element.

The whole range of indexes all together is known as a slice of several elements.

Finding Your Specific Index Number (Indexing)

To find an item corresponding to a given index number, the first thing that you will need to do is write the name of the string, followed by the index number in brackets.

```
>>>mystring = "truly, madly, deeply"
>>>mystring[2]
'u'
```

Finding a Particular Array of Data (Slicing)

The technique of slicing allows to you find items in a specified slice. The slice expression here is as follows:

Beginning of the slice: end of the slice

This generally means that you want to get the data up to but not including the specified number.

Focusing on the previous example:

```
>>>mystring[7:12]
'madly'
```

Two handy tips about slicing which you might findinteresting.Here we will be using the string alpha = "abcde" for the following two tips:

- If you somehow accidently use an index number that is greater that the length of your string, you will get an indexError:

```
>>> alpha[10]
Traceback (most recent call last):
        File "<stdin>", line 1, in
<module>
IndexError: string index out of
range
```

- When counting from left to right, we are always using positive numbers. If you want to do a negative indexing, then you can use negative numbers to count from right to left.

```
>>> alpha[-1]
        'e'
```

Creating New Strings from Presently Immutable Strings

Yes, it is actually possible to do that. You can use a combination of Slicing and the concatenation operator (+) to break down immutable (unchangeable) strings and generate new ones from them.

```
>>> candy = 'dark chocolate bars'
>>>morecandy = 'milk' + candy[4:]
>>> print morecandy
milk chocolate bars
```

String Formatting: The Big Cheese of String Manipulation

In the long run, formatting strings might turn into a very crucial and essential tool for your day to day work time. While there are many ways through which strings can be formatted, the most common method is using the % operator which is also known as the interpolation operator.

For those of you who might be unaware of this concept, the word "formatting" basically means us specifying what happens whenever a value is inserted into a string. For example, we might want to specify how many digits are needed to be displayed after a certain decimal point. That will be formatting.

Understand The Formatting Codes

The following is a list of the available formatting codes. The sequence is to first use the % operator followed by the "Conversion Type" required.

See the following example, which seamlessly determines the precision level of the constant pi (how many digits are required after the decimal point).

```
>>> import math
>>> "The value of pi is about %.10f"
% math.pi
        'The value of pi is about
3.1415926536'
```

- **%s:** This is perhaps the most widely used code. Its function is to convert any Python data you enter into a string.
- **%c:** This works with a single character.
- **%d, %i:** This works with an integer decimal.
- **%f:** This goes for floating point decimals.
- **% %:**The percent sign is essentially to act as an escape character for using a real percent sign.

```
>>> "50%% of nothing is still %i" %
0
        '50% of nothing is still 0'
```

Formatting Something with Just a Single Data Item

If, for example, you have a single data point and you want that to be included in your string, you will need to follow the given steps.

Here we will be inserting the data, **mystring = "swallow"**

- Firstly, type the new string up to the point where you want your data to be inserted.

```
>>>> "An African or European
```

- Next, write the formatting code of (%s) which means that you are going to be inserting a new string data.

```
>>>> "An African or European %s
```

- After that is done, you will need to enter the mystring value as follows.

```
>>> "An African or European %s?" %
mystring
         'An African or European
swallow?'
```

Chapter Four: Study Questions

Q1) What is the function of double quotes?

a) Allows you to encapsulate a string

b) Allows you to encapsulate an integer

c) Allows you to encapsulate a boolean value

d) Allows you to encapsulate a double value

Answer: A

Q2) What does a triple Quote do?

a) Allows you encapsulate a normal string

b) Allows you to print a multi lined string, retaining the format

c) Allows you to print a multi lined string without retaining the format

d) Creates a documentation of the encapsulated string

Answer: B

Q3) What does putting "\" as last character on a line mean?

a) Backlash

b) Linefeed

c) Tab

d) Text on the next line goes with the text on the prior line

Answer: D

Q4) What does \e mean ?

a) Linefeed

b) Escape key

c) Tab

d) Backlash

Answer: B

Q5) What does the method (endswith) do?

a) It checks for a specified content at the of a string

b) It adds a specified content at the ends of a string

c) It removes a specified content from the end of a string

d) It alters the end of a string with a specified content

Answer: A

Chapter Five: The Lists and the Tuples!

If you have been involved with any sort of programming, then the concept of Lists and Tuples will immediately feel very familiar to you, as they are very similar to Arrays. For those of you who are not, let us explain.

Lists and Tuples are basically Python's compound data types. This means that they act as a container and hold a collection of data.

Both Lists and Tuples can very easily be manipulated through indexing or slicing. The elements inside these are generally numbered sequentially, starting from 0. So you can see that the manipulations of these are similar to that of strings.

What is a List / Tuple?

A list in terms of Python is a mutable data type, which essentially means that the contents of said list can be altered without the generation of another list. A list can hold strings, numbers, tuples – and these are powerful enough to even contain classes or functions!

Below is an example of a list:

```
a_list = ['this', 'is', 'a', 'list']
empty_list = []
another_list = [5]
```

Tuples, on the other hand, are generally the same thing as lists, with the exception that these are immutable and can contain lots of different elements of different data types.

Deciding Which One to Choose

Since both of them are essentially the same thing, sometimes it might be a little bit difficult to choose which one to go with. Bear in mind that there are some very glaring intrinsic differences between the two:

- Tuples are essentially immutable while lists are mutable
- In terms of memory efficiency, Tuples takes the crown
- Lists have lots of useful built-in methods

So, considering the above data, sometimes it might get a little tricky to choose which one might be suitable for your current work. Python's creator himself (Guido) has promoted some very simplistic conventions which are recommended to be followed when choosing between Lists and Tuples:

- Tuples are suitable for heterogeneous data and sequence keys, and some specific functions that require argument to be passed in tuples.
- Lists are suitable for homogenous data and mutable objects.

Defining A List/Tuple

When trying to declare a Tuple literal, you should keep in mind that it can be defined in one of the following three ways:

- It can have a single element followed by a comma
- It can have multiple elements separated by commas
- It can also be a set of empty parentheses

Below we have given few examples of tuples:

```
>>>a_tuple = ('this', 'is', 'a',
'tuple')
>>> tuple_2 = "this", "is",
"another", "tuple"
>>> tuple_2
('this', 'is', 'another', 'tuple')
>>>empty_tuple = ()
```

Converting Any Object to a Tuple

For this you will need to use a tuple() function:

```
>>>mylist = [1, 2, 3]
>>> tuple(mylist)
(1, 2, 3)
```

Manipulation of Sequence Objects

The sections in this area will tell you about the various ways through which you can manipulate data in your tuples.

Object Comparison Between Sequence

Comparison	Reason
(1, 2, 3) < (1, 2, 4), [1, 2, 3] < [1, 2, 4]	3 is less than 4
'ABC' < 'C' < 'Pascal' < 'Python'	ASCII order of characters
(1, 2, 4) > (1, 2, 3, 4), (1, 2) < (1, 2, -1)	First sequence is the same as the beginning of second sequence
(1, 2, 3) == (1.0, 2.0, 3.0)	Integers equal their float equivalents
(1, 2, ('aa', 'ab')) < (1, 2, ('abc', 'a'), 4)	Alphabetical order of characters in sub-sequence ('aa' is smaller than 'abc')

Comparisons between sequences are done if the objects in question are of the same data type. When a comparison is done the result tells whether or not any specified data is smaller or larger than another one. The convention through which this is done is as follows:

77

- The first element of the sequence is always compared with the second one.
- If a situation arises where an item inside a sequence is a sequence itself, then each of the elements in the sequence is compared against the other element of the corresponding sequence.
- If all the items in any two given sequences are equal, then they are equal.
- Strings are always compared based on the ASCII order of representing characters.

Sequence Object Manipulation

- Addition: The (+) operator combines the element of multiple lists together to create a list, and combines tuples together to create a tuple.

```
>>> [1, 2, 3] + [2, 4]
[ 1 , 2, 3, 2, 4]
```

- **Sequence Multiplication:** The (*) operator is responsible for repeating the contents of a list or tuple.

- **Augmented Assignment:** The += and *= falls under this category. They simultaneously concatenate and assign– or repeat and assign – a value to a list or tuple, depending on which one is used.

- **Comparison Operators:** These include < , > , ==, != operators, which test the elements of two or more tuples.

- **Content Test:** The "in" keyword is used to check if any specified element is present in a list or tuple.

```
>>>phone_sounds = ('beep', 'ring',
'flight of the bumblebee')
>>> y = 'beep' in phone_sounds
>>> y
  True
```

Creating a List Copy

The list() function present in Python will allow you to create a copy of the specified list. It will also allow you to turn any other sequence or object or iterable into a new list.

```
>>>mytuple = ('apple', 'orange',
'pear')
>>>mylist = list(mytuple)
```

```
>>>mylist
['apple', 'orange', 'pear'
```

Add an Element at the End of a List

Using the append () method, you will be able to do just that!
Let's have a look at an example where 'apple' is added to the
beginning of an already created list.

```
basket = ['apple', 'banana',
'orange']
basket.append('apple')
```

Add a List to the Contents of Another
Sequence

For this action, we will need to call the method extend().
Please note that if the iterable is a string, then each of the
characters will be added separately.

Here in the example. We are going to add the characters of
'pear':

```
>>> x = ['apple', 'apple', 'banana',
'orange']
>>>x.extend('pear')
>>> x
```

```
['apple', 'apple', 'banana',
'orange', 'p', 'e', 'a', 'r']
```

To Delete a Value from a Sequence

For that we are going to need to use the remove() method.

```
>>>x.remove('apple')
>>> x
['apple', 'banana', 'orange', 'p',
'e', 'a', 'r']
```

Sorting and Reversing

We have already talked a little bit about the sort method, which sorts out the elements of the list according to their ASCII code values. The reverse() method, on the other hand, as the name implies, reverses the whole list.

```
>>>x.sort()
>>> x
['a', 'apple', 'banana', 'e',
'orange', 'p', 'r']
>>>x.reverse()
>>> x
['r', 'p', 'orange', 'e', 'banana',
'apple', 'a']
```

Indexing and Slicing of Lists

We have already discussed how Index numbers work in conjunction with strings. A similar theory applies here as well when dealing with Lists and Tuples. For example, the code below shows the item stored at Index number 0 and 1 from the list x.

```
>>> x = ['apple', 'banana', 'pear']
>>> x[0]
'apple'
>>> x[1]
'banana
```

When brought into comparison, however, it should be noted that there is a slight difference between the indexing of strings and that of lists, mainly because lists are mutable. The data of the list itself can be changed by slicing and indexing, but this cannot be done in either a string or Tuple.

Retrieve Data from a List

For this you should keep the following syntax in mind.

```
sequence_object_name[firstindex:last
index:step]
```

In the example below, we are creating a list of numbers and then applying the slice index to bring out all the even numbers.

```
>>>mylist = range(0,10)
>>>mylist[::2]
[0, 2, 4, 6, 8]
```

Altering a List Item

This can be done in a number of ways, but one of the simplest is to assign elements to a list by using index numbers.

- First state the name of the list where you would like your item to go as well as the index number.

```
mylist[1]
```

- Next, assign the element that you want to add using a = sign.

- In the following example, we are replacing the string "eggs" with the string "love spam". Note that "eggs" is situated at index 1.

```
>>> L = ['spam', 'eggs', 'ham']
>>> L[1] = 'lovely spam'
>>> L
['spam', 'lovely spam', 'ham']
```

Returning an Index Number

If you want to know the index number of an element, you are to use the index() method:

```
>>>mylist = [1, 'two', 3]
>>>mylist.index('two')
1
```

Insert an Item Before a Particular Index Number

For this action, you are going to need to call upon the insert() method:

```
>>>basket.insert(0, 'peach')
>>> basket
['peach', 'apple', 'banana',
'orange']
```

Remove a Specific Item and Return to Your Designated Index Number

For this action you are going to use the pop() method, as follows:

```
>>> breakfast = ['spam', 'spam',
'spam', 'baked beans', 'spam',
'spam']
>>>breakfast.pop(3)
  'baked beans'
>>> breakfast
  ['spam', 'spam', 'spam', 'spam',
'spam']
```

Building Incremental Lists

Since lists are mutable, you have the option to build the lists through just one element at a time, which is often really useful as it allows you to build lists from other iterable objects, or congregate different parts of multiple lists. The best way to do this is use the for loop and apply the previously mentioned append() method as below:

```
L1 = ['spam', 'spam', 'spam', 'baked
beans', None, 'spam', 'spam']
L2 = []
for i in L1:
```

```
if i is not None:
L2.append(i)
```

Stacks and Queues

The first thing that you should keep in mind here is that Stacks and Queues are not necessarily objects of Python, but the versatility of Python allows lists to be coded in such a way that they uphold the properties of either Stacks or Queues.

The main difference between these two is that a Stack basically works like a spring-loaded slingshot, where the last item is the first item to get flung off. Queue, on the other hand, follows the standard procedure of "First come first served," and as such, the first item is the first item to be interacted with.

Adding to Stacks

To add anything on top of a stack, use the append () method. In the following example, we are going to place six plates on a pile.

```
>>> plates = [ ]
>>> for p in range(6):
... plates.append(p)
...
```

```
>>> plates
```

```
[0, 1, 2, 3, 4, 5]
```

Retrieve Item from Top

This is as simple as using the pop() method. By default it will retrieve the last item (since it's a stack).

```
>>> while plates:
... plates.pop()
...
5

4

3

2

1

0
```

Adding to Queue

The same procedure as Stacks is followed when adding to a Queue, but here the element will be added at the end.

```
>>> callers = []
>>> for c in range(6):
... callers.append(c)
...
>>> callers
[0, 1, 2, 3, 4, 5]
```

Retrieving from Queue

Similarly, for retrieving from a Queue, we will be using the while loop starting with pop (0)

```
3. >>> while callers:
4. ... callers.pop(0)
5. ...
6. 0
7. 1
8. 2
9. 3
10.4
11.5
```

Chapter Five: Study Questions

Q1) A Tuple is –

a) A list of data whose contents are static

b) A list of data whose contents are changeable

c) A singular data which cannot be changed

d) A singular data that can be changed

Answer: A

Q2) Which of the following is correct?

a)   Both list and Tuples hold mutable data

b) Lists are more memory efficient than Tuples

c) Tuples have a lot of built-in methods

d) Lists have a lot of built-in methods

Answer: C

Q3) Which of the following code will allow you to convert an object to Tuple?

a) >>> mylist = [1, 2, 3]

>>> convert.tuple(mylist)

(1, 2, 3)

b) >>> mylist = [1, 2, 3]

>>> alter.tuple(mylist)

(1, 2, 3)

c) >>> mylist = [1, 2, 3]

>>> changetotuple(mylist)

(1, 2, 3)

d) >>> mylist = [1, 2, 3]

>>> tuple(mylist)

(1, 2, 3)

Answer: D

Q4) Which of the following ASCII order of character is true?

a) 'ABC < 'C' < 'Pascal ' < ' Python'

b) 'ABC <= 'C' <= 'Pascal ' <= ' Python'

c) 'ABC > 'C' > 'Pascal ' >' Python'

d) 'ABC' ='C' = 'Pascal ' = ' Python'

Answer: A

Q5) < , > and == are :

a) Content Testers

b) Sequence Multipliers

c) Arithmetic Operators

d) Comparison Operators

Answer: D

Chapter Six: Bringing Control Over Your Program

We have talked a little bit about control structures in previous chapters. These are specific codes that are used to set up conditions and determine if a chunk of code should run; and, if it should run, then how many times it should run. We have talked about the comparison operators, which are also a type of control statement. In this chapter we will focus on the more advanced ones such as for/while loops and also the if operator.

The If Operator

The if statement gives Python the instruction to carry out an action only and only if the given condition is true. Here, comparison operators (covered in a previous chapter) are used to set up the condition. The result will come in the form of either yes or no, hence these are called Boolean comparisons.

Writing the If Statement

To properly employ the If statement in your program, see the example below.

- First, type the if and then a condition, followed by a colon:

```
if weather == "raining":
```

- Next, you will need to type in the instruction or condition that will be required for the statement to be valid:

```
if weather == "raining":
bring_umbrella = "yes"
```

Adding an Extra Condition to If Block

Believe it or not, it is actually possible to test for several conditions at once in Python by adding up extra chunks of code as "additional blocks" to the already stated if statement. These blocks begin with the keyword **elif.**

In order to apply these, you will need to follow these instructions.

- First write the if statement as taught above:

```
if weather == "raining":
bring_umbrella = "yes"
```

- Next, instead of indenting, in the immediate next line, you are going to type elif followed by a condition and another colon:

```
    if weather == "raining":
bring_umbrella = "yes"
elif weather == "windy":
```

- Then, in the immediate next line, indent just four spaces and type in your new instruction:

```
if weather == "raining":
bring_umbrella = "yes"
elif weather == "windy":
bring_jacket = "yes"
```

The Power of the Else Statement

Now that you know about the If statement, you are going to need to have a good deal of knowledge on the Else statement, as this block usually describes the final instruction to be followed if none of the preceding conditions were met.

- First write the if statement as shown above.
- If you have any additional conditions to be declared, declare them using the elif statement.

- Once done, on the next line add else:
- Go to the next line, give four space indents and then type your instruction!

```
go_out = "now! what are you waiting
for?"
```

The final code should look something like this:

```
if weather == "raining":
bring_umbrella = "yes"
elif weather == "windy":
bring_jacket = "yes"
else:
go_out = "now! what are you waiting
for?"
```

A Pro Tip: Combining Multiple Tests

Sure, you can always pile up multiple elif statements for multiple conditions. But there's a shortcut that allows you to perform the same action in just one statement by combining the if and elif statements.

Have look at the sample using elif block:

```
if age < 18:
     print "Discount rate"
elif age > 65:
     print "Discount rate"
else:
     print "Adult rate"
```

Now look at the same problem with just an if statement and two conditions:

```
if (age < 18) or (age > 65):
print "Discount rate"
else:
print "Adult rate
```

The For Loop

Unlike human beings, who often find doing the same thing over and over again tedious and drab, computers are quiet adept at it. And to utilize this feature, you will need to learn how to use Loops. Here, we will discuss the features of a For loop.

A very basic example of a For loop goes like this:

```
for mychar in "hello!":
print "the ascii value of", mychar,
"is", ord(mychar)

the ascii value of h is 104
the ascii value of e is 101
the ascii value of l is 108
the ascii value of l is 108
the ascii value of o is 111
the ascii value of ! is 33
```

The program which you just saw is designed to print out the ASCII value of all of the characters in the word "hello." We achieve this by combining the For loop with the ord() function.

Compatibility of the For Loop

It should be kept in mind now that a For loop only works with objects in Python that contain more than one element inside them. Such data are called iterables.

Below are the kinds of objects with which the For loop of Python is compatible.

```
for element in range(1,4): # range
    print element
```

```
for element in [1, 2, 3]: # list
        print element
for key in {'one':1, 'two':2}: #
dictionary
        print key
for line in open("myfile.txt"): #
text fileprint line
for value in mydict.itervalues(): #
iterator object
        print value
for key, value in
mydict.iteritems(): # tuple
unpacking
        print key, value
```

Setting the Range of Your For Loop

Whenever you are setting up a For loop, it is almost certain that you might want your loop to go through a specific range of numbers. To do that, you will need to use the range() function as follows:

```
>>> range(10)
[0, 1, 2, 3, 4, 5, 6, 7, 8, 9]
```

Alternatively, you can also use thexrange() function, which is pretty much the same thing as the range() function – with the slight difference in the fact that it returns an iterator object instead of a list that creates the number within the given range.

To clarify the difference, look at the example below:

```
>>> range(0, 10, 3)
[0, 3, 6, 9]
>>>xrange(0, 10, 3)
xrange(0, 12, 3)
```

More appropriately, if you want to implement your range or xrange functionalities in a list, you will need to do the following:

- First create a while loop (discussed soon)
- Then create a new list as follows:

```
>>>man_from_st_ives = ['wives',
'sacks', 'cats', 'kits']
>>>newlist = []
>>> for i in man_from_st_ives:
... newlist += ['7', i]
...
>>>newlist
```

```
['7', 'wives', '7', 'sacks', '7',
'cats', '7', 'kits']
```

The While Loop

Unlike the For loop, the While loop is designed in such a way that it is able to perform an action infinite times, as long as the given condition remains satisfied.

For writing a While loop, you will need to follow these steps:

- First write while, followed by a Boolean expression and then by a colon:

```
while number_of_bottles> 0:
```

- Next, you are going to want to leave four spaces and type the instruction that you want to be carried out:

```
        while number_of_bottles> 0:
                print
number_of_bottles, "bottles of beer
on the wall"
```

99

While loops can be used to create very complex programs that require user inputs as well. Have a look at the coin toss code below that utilizes both the If and While control statements.

```python
import random
headcount = tailcount = 0
userinput = ''
print "Now tossing a coin..."
while userinput.lower() != "q":
    flip = random.choice(['heads',
    'tails'])
    if flip == 'heads':
        headcount += 1
        print "heads! the number of heads is
now %d" % headcount
    else:
        tailcount += 1
        print "tails! the number of tails is
now %d" % tailcount
    print "Press 'q' to quit",
    userinput = raw_input("or another
key to toss again:")
print "the total number of heads:",
headcount
print "the total number of tails:",
tailcount
```

Some Useful Loop Statements

Using a loop might be a little bit complicated at first, but below we have given a few useful statements that should help you in the long run.

The Break

Whenever you might find yourself in a pickle, needing to escape from a loop, use the break keyword which stops the processing of the loop and exits it. Any code present after the break statement will be ignored.

```
>>> y = "astring"
>>> for i in y:
... if i == 'n':
... print "broke!"
... break
... print i,
... print "*",
...
a * s * t * r * i * broke
```

The Continue

Opposite to the break keyword, the continue statement, if found in the middle of a loop, will cause the loop to skip the rest of the code after the continue keyword and run the loop from the beginning.

```
>>> for n in range(10):
... if n == 5:
... print "five",
... print n,
...
0 1 2 3 4 five 5 6 7 8 9
```

The Pass

The pass keyword, on the other hand, tells Python to do absolutely nothing. This is a keyword that is mostly used in classes, but it can also be used in While or For loops as well.

```
>>>defargument_clinic(minutes):
... if minutes >= 5:
... pass
... else:
... print "No it isn't!"
...
>>> minutes = 4
>>>argument_clinic(minutes)
No it isn't!
>>> minutes = 5
>>>argument_clinic(minutes) #
```

```
nothing happens
>>>
```

The Reversal

The reversed () function works to return an iterator, which works through the given sequence of items completely backwards. This feature is pretty new as it joins the Python family after version 2.4.

```
for f in reversed(range(1, 11)):
print f,
print "blastoff!"

10 9 8 7 6 5 4 3 2 1 blastoff!
```

Sorting

The sorted() function here is used to return a list that is fully sorted, while keeping the source completely untouched.

```
>>>mylist = [1, 10, 2, 9, 3, 8, 4,
7, 5, 6]
>>>mynewlist = sorted(mylist)
>>>mynewlist
[1, 2, 3, 4, 5, 6, 7, 8, 9, 10]
>>>mylist # original list is
```

```
unchanged
[1, 10, 2, 9, 3, 8, 4, 7, 5, 6]
```

Deciding the Correct Loop

Now that you pretty much know about the functions of both the While and For loop, you might be thinking: Which loop will be the best one to use? The thing here is that there is no one divine loop suitable for every situation. Instead you are going to need to assess the scenario before deciding which one to use. The following should help you in doing that.

Good Scenarios for a For Loop

- When you need to iterate through a sequence one item at a time.
- When you need a loop to be repeated for a fixed number of times.
- When you are going through a text file.

Good Uses for the While Loop

- For programs that are event-driven and require the user's input to justify the next action to be taken.
- When a situation requires you to process a container object while modifying it at the same time.

Chapter Six: Study Questions

Q1) Which of the following is an example of an IF statement

a) if weather == raining:

    bring_umbrella = "yes"

b) if weather == "raining":

    bring_umbrella = "yes"

c) if weather =! "raining":

    bring_umbrella = "yes"

d) if weather == "raining":

    bring_umbrella = _yes

Answer: B

Q2) A While loop is a loop which:

a) Keeps carrying out an operation infinitely beyond a specified condition

b) Keeps carrying out an operation until it has met a specific condition

c) A loop that cannot take any conditions

d) All of the above

Answer: A

Q3) What is the function of break?

a) It stops the loop and omits the rest of the code

b) It corrupts the program

c) It exits the loop and stops the processing of the loop

d) None of the above

Answer: C

Q4) What does the sorted() function do?

a) It jumbles up a sorted list

b) It arranges items in descending order

c) It arranges items in ascending order

d) None of the above

Answer: C

Q5) Which one of the following is a good scenario to use FOR loop

a) For programs that are event driven and require user input

b) For situation where you are required to process a container object while modifying it

c) When you are needed to iterate through a sequence one item at a time

d) None of the above

Answer: C

Chapter Seven: Working In-Depth with Functions

So, Functions in Python are basically specific blocks of code that are written to perform a specific action while returning a result. This chapter is going to deal with this topic as a whole.

Some Benefits of Using Functions

- Using functions will allow you to write various codes only once and re-use them throughout the program or any other program.

- Using functions helps to keep the program simple by hiding all of the unnecessary elements of a program, making it easier for the user to understand.

- Since the usage of functions minimizes complexity, it allows you to organize your program much more logically.

How to Call a Function

Don't worry; you won't have to dial a number here. In the world of programming, using a function is referred as calling a function. For that you will need to perform the following actions:

- Type a name where the result of the function is to be held followed by an (=) sign.
- Carve in the name of the function.
- In the further parentheses, fill in the information required for your function to work.

Defining a Function

Now that you know how to call a function, let us show you how to define one.

Keep in mind that the following instructions are only applicable when you are not calling a built-in function.

- The first step for defining a function is to write the word def and the name of the function. In the parentheses, add the names of the parameters on which the function will act, separating them with commas. Finally, put in a colon to end the statement.

```
defmy_function(arg1, arg2):
```

- Next you will need to write the function of the code. Make sure to indent each line of code with four spaces. A finished function code might look like this:

```
defmy_function(arg1, arg2):
    """

    my function does this
    """
    do something
    if this:
    do that
    return something else
```

One thing you can note here is that once your function definition is complete, you can give your function a new name. This name can be perhaps an easier name to call the function throughout your program.

```
>>>tinyfunction
<function tinyfunction at 0x61430>
>>>myfunc = tinyfunction

>>>myfunc
<function tinyfunction at 0x61430>
```

An optional technique, but highly important, is to add doc strings to your functions. These are essentially the first code in a function in a string form. It can span throughout multiple lines and act as a guideline letting the users know what the function is all about.

```
defprintme(me):
print me
```

Returning a Value from a Function

Since you have now learned how to define and use a function, the following section will show you the codes on how you will be able to return a value from a function.

- The first thing which you should do here is include a return statement in your function as such:

```
defmy_function(b):
a = b + 42
return a
```

- Use your function in an expression:

```
my_value = my_function(3)
```

- The above code means that the returned value of my_function has now been assigned to my_value. The final code should look as such:

```
>>>my_value = my_function(3)
>>> print my_value
          45
```

Introducing Parameters

Parameters are basically empty containers or placeholders for various types of information, which you can provide in order to make your function perform a specific action.

There are multiple ways through which a parameter can be introduced to a function. We will be covering a few here. But before that, there are some key points that you should know about functional parameters:

- A function is able to hold any number of parameters.
- When a function is defined, the number of parameters it will hold is also defined.
- It is possible to assign default values to your parameters.
- Whenever you are calling a function, the parameters are passed.

- A parameter can be recalled as being a literal or as a name.
- Parameters are actually called arguments.

Specifying an Argument When Calling a Function

This is the most generic way through which you will be able to specify an argument for your function. The method is to pass the argument to your function while calling them.

The argument to be passed needs to be typed inside parentheses of the function as such:

```
>>>a_function(myarg)
```

Have a look at the following example to further clarify the concept. Here the example creates a function that prints the value of its argument while giving a name to a tuple and passing the name to the function.

```
>>>defa_function(x):
... print "you passed me the
argument", repr(x)
...
>>>myarg = (1,2,3)
```

```
>>>a_function(myarg)
you passed me the argument (1, 2, 3
```

Specifying Arguments Using Keywords

In some cases, you will be able define a function with default values for parameters. These are called keyword arguments. To create such arguments, these are the steps that you will have to follow:

- First type any parameters that are not destined to have a keyword.

- Then type the argument in the form keyword = value.

In the example below, the function has been defined as one requiring a positional parameter and two default value parameters:

```
defrecipes(ingredient, servings=4,
mode="Vegetarian"):
```

Alternatively, when you will be calling a function that includes default-value parameters, you will need to follow these rules:

- Pass all the values of positional parameters first.

- Next, pass the values or names of any default values whose pre-defined values you want to change.

Some Tips to Remember While Assigning Arguments Using Keywords

Below is some very basic knowledge that you should carry with you in order to avoid some silly mistakes new programmers often make while assigning argumentative keywords.

- Never pass data for default-value parameters whose values might be useful to you later on. The following example is of such a mistake where the function uses both of the default values:

```
>>>recipes('shiitake mushrooms')
```

- If you want to include default value parameters anyway in the order following which they were defined, you can simply pass them as shown here:

```
>>>recipes('arugula', 8,
"Carnivore")
```

- Always keep in mind that immutable default values always remain the same because Python always evaluates all the default values in a function definition just once. That is when the function itself is defined, (def is first run). Have a look at the example below. Even though mynum is changed, Python still uses the previous value.

```
>>>mynum = 8            # Integers are
immutable.
>>>def f(arg=mynum):
... return arg
...
>>> f()
8

>>>mynum = 10
# We're
>>> f()
# ...but the function still uses 8.
8
```

- Keep in mind that Assignments (=) always result in a specific name referring to another object, even if the object is mutable. Therefore, unlike the append() method, this does not congregate arguments.

```
>>>def f(q, mylist=[]):
...             mylist = mylist + q
...             return mylist
...
>>> a = [1]
>>> f(a)
[1]
>>> a = [2]
>>> f(a)
[2]
```

- Working directly on a mutable object is a very bad idea, as the arguments might bear many unexpected results. It's therefore always better to work on a copy of the object. The following example creates a new copy of a list and then assigns a value to each of the elements:

```
def f(mylist, data):
newlist = mylist[:] # make a copy of
mylist
for i in range(len(mylist)):
newlist[i] = mylist[i] + data
return newlist
```

As you can see here, if the above function is called once again, the values of the original list remains untouched.

```
>>>alist = [1, 2, 3]
>>> x = f(alist, 5)
>>> print x
[6, 7, 8]
>>> print alist
[1, 2, 3]
```

Chapter Seven: Study Questions

Q1) Which one of the following might be a good time call a function?

a) A situation where you might need to make the program more complex

b) A situation where you are willing to write various codes only once and use them throughout the program continuously

c) A situation where you are going to want to expose different unnecessary elements to the user for debugging

d) None of the above

Answer: B

Q2) The information required for a function to work are kept inside:

a) Second brackets

b) Asterisk

c) Third Brackets

d) Parenthesis

Answer: D

Q3) Which of the following will return a value from a function?

a) def my_function(b):

   a = b + 42

   collect a

b) def my_function(b):

   a = b + 42

   return a

c) def my_function(b):

   a = b + 42

   send a

d) def my_function(b):

   a = b + 42

   give a

Answer: B

Q4) Which of the following is true about function parameters?

a) A function is able to hold only limited number parameters

b) A function can be defined without defining the number of parameters held

c) When a function is called, a parameter is never passed

d) Parameters are actually called arguments

Answer: D

Chapter Eight: Introduction to Classes and Object Oriented Programming

A programming book can never be complete without a chapter wholly dedicated to classes, now can it? All of the big-boy programming languages out there hold a great chunk of their functionality in the Object Oriented aspect of programming and Python is no different. So, let's dive in!

The first thing that you should know here is what classes are. These are basically tools for creating new types of objects in Python. Whenever we are creating a class, we are also assigning a data and behavior to that object. Or inside a suitcase!

Programs created using these suitcases as foundations are much easier to manipulate and customize.

The Basic Concepts of Object Oriented Programming

So, before we start teaching you the actual creation process of OOP, we would like you to understand some of the core concepts of OOP that will allow you to better grasp the deeper topics which we are going to cover.

Object Oriented Programming is basically Python's way of handling objects which are, simply put, suitcases or bundles containing encapsulated data and methods.

Objects

In OOP, an object simply refers to an encapsulated form that can hold any data, information or behavior (action) you might like.

As an example:

- Consider a dog. It belongs to a breed (breed is the class and dog is the object).
- If the dog has a name tag, then it probably has a name and age associated with it. (these are the attributes or data)
- The dog has actions (behaviors) such as running, eating, and sleeping.

The Concepts of Inheriting, Overriding and Extending

Here you should understand that a class is not a standalone thing in Python. From one class, which acts as parent, it is possible to pull out a number of subclasses.

When these subclasses are formed, they inherit the behavior and action properties of the parent class. This is called inheriting.

When the subclass tries to create or alter the way the parent class is working, it is called overriding a property.

And finally, when the subclass tries to introduce new data or methods that are not present in the parent class, it is said that it is extending the parent class.

The Concept of Polymorphism

In the simplest of terms, polymorphism is a general feature of almost all OOP languages which allows routines to use different types of variables at different times.

Specifically speaking about Python, here polymorphism is based on names. Assuming that there is an object named file, it can have three rudimentary methods. Namely: read () , write () and close(). Now, if you create a new class containing those three methods, even that won't be a file object, you will still be able to create instances of your class and apply them to places where Python might be expecting to receive a file type object.

A Look at Class and Instances

We have talked about classes and subclasses but we didn't really explain what a class is. So, here it is: a class is nothing but a general description of something, a template if you will.

And instances are objects created from the class using the attributes and methods described in the class itself.

Say for example that you have a copy of the famous American Kennel Club breed standard for a Labrador retriever. Here, the AKC is the class that describes the basic attributes and abilities of a Labrador. In Python terms, such a class might look like:

```
class Lab:
weight = 60 # data attribute
def retrieve(self, thing): # method
attribute
return(thing)
```

An instance, as mentioned earlier, is simply a copy made from the previously specified template. So, you can think of it as your own personal pet, having all of the properties as described in the AKC.

In Python, the code for this would be:

```
>>> pilot = Lab()
```

The Attributes

After an instance is created, anything that you declare inside the class –be it a method, information or any other kind of code – becomes an attribute of the class itself.

To check the attribute of a class, all you need to do is write the name of the class/instance, put a dot, and then punch in the attribute name:

```
>>>Lab.weight
60
>>>pilot.weight
60
```

Creating Classes

In this section, we will learn how to write and call a class while creating an instance of it. Throughout this section, we will be focusing on this example.

```
class NameTag:
def __init__(self, myname):
self.myname = myname
def say(self):
print "Hello, my name is",
self.myname
```

Creating A Class

Creating a class is pretty simple. The format is you have to type class, the name of the class followed by a colon.

```
class NameTag:
```

How To Write an __init__() method

Most classes out there have a built-in __init__() method, which acts like a constructor, and it runs whenever you create an instance of that class. It typically pre-determines how many arguments the instance is going to need and puts the instance into a default state.

Some key points that you should keep in mind when considering an __init__() method are:

- The __init__() method is a very special kind of method dubbed as initialize. The two underscores are what Python uses to determine a special method.
- It is almost a convention for __init__() method to come first in a class.

The basic syntax of this method is:

```
>>>def __init__(self)
```

Writing an __init__() with attribute

Very soon, you will need to write various classes that will pass arguments when making instances from them. In case of __init__(), creating attributes for such parameters will make it easier for other methods to interact with them.

- The first thing that you want to do is put a four space indent beneath your class definition header:

```
def __init__(self
```

- On the exact same line, go with a comma and write the parameter name:

```
def __init__(self, myname
```

- Keep repeating process two until you have written all the names of your required parameters, and close it with a colon and end brackets:

```
def __init__(self, myname):
```

- The next step is to go to the next line and put a four space indent past the def statement.

- Create another attribute that goes by the name of self, put a dot and do the following:

```
def __init__(self, myname
self.myname = myname
```

Writing Other Methods in a Class

The __init __() method is normally used just to give initial information about the class itself. But if you want to create your own methods, this how you would do that.

- First, make sure to leave a four indent space, then type def and the name of the method and (self:

```
defsay(self
```

- End the line by typing):

- After that, you can indent four more spaces and type in more codes for your function.

```
def say(self):
print "Hello, my name is",
self.myname
```

Creating Class Attributes

It is possible to put any code or form of assignments into a class. Any information put inside a class automatically becomes its attribute.

```
class NameTag:
favorite_color = "Blue"
```

After which, if we go ahead and try to generate an instance of the said class, we will see that the instance also has the attribute that we created:

```
>>>grail_seeker =
NameTag('lancelot')
>>>grail_seeker.favorite_color
'Blue'
```

Create an Instance

For you to create an instance of a class, you will need to follow
the below steps.

- First type the name of your instance with an equal sign:

```
hello =
```

- Next type the name of class and add a (

```
        hello = NameTag(
```

- If you want to add parameters, then this would be the
  time add them as well:

```
        hello = NameTag('Arthur'
```

- Finally finalize the code with:

```
hello = NameTag('Arthur')
```

Subclass Creation

We have already discussed what classes and subclasses are. If you want to create a subclass out of a class, all you will need to do is type class, then the name of your subclass, and top it off with the name of the superclass (parent class) from which it is inherited.

```
class GeekNameTag(NameTag):
```

Overriding Superclass Methods

It is possible to create a subclass that will overwrite the methods of the parent class, as discussed at the beginning of the chapter; such a class can be created using the following code.

In this example, we are creating a say() method that will behave differently from that of the parent class's say() method.

```
class GeekNameTag(NameTag):
def say(self):
```

```
        print "The current value of
my name is", self.myname
```

Extension of a Superclass Method

There are technically two ways through which it is possible to extend a superclass method.

By Extending an Existing Superclass Method

For this, you will need to follow the steps below:

- First, you will need to define a method with an identical name as the superclass method from which you wish to extend.

```
        class
WeirdGreeting(NameTag):

def say(self):
```

- Next, while writing the method's code, you will need to call upon the superclass method by giving it the name, followed by a dot, of the method name and the argument.

```
class WeirdGreeting(NameTag):
def say(self):

NameTag.say(self)
```

In the example given below, we are extending a the say() method of NameTag:

```
class WeirdGreeting(NameTag):
def say(self):
        NameTag.say(self)
        printself.myname.swapcase()
```

After it's done, you will be able to call it using the code:

```
>>> greet = WeirdGreeting('Totoro')
>>>greet.say()
Hello, my name is Totoro
tOTORO
```

Extending a Superclass Method by Adding a New Method

You also have the option here to write a completely new subclass method that will add a brand new behavior to your parent class. In the example below, we are creating a new subclass called NameTag and creating a method that is extending the parent class by saving the NameTag in the database.

```
class PersistentNameTag(NameTag):
def save(self):
        db.write(pickle.dumps(self))
```

Chapter Eight: Study Questions

Q1) What is a class?

a) Classes are blueprints from which no object can be created

b) Classes are blueprints whose properties are inherited to an object created from that class

c) Classes are blueprints whose properties cannot be inherited by an object created from that class

d) None of the above

Answer: B

Q2) What is an object?

a) An object refers to an encapsulation of data, information or behavior

b) An object refers to a random function

c) An object refers to an encapsulation of only behavior

d) None of the above

Answer: A

Q3) What is the concept of overriding?

a) It is the process where a sub-class is created from a parent class

b) It is the process where a sub-class inherits behavior and action from parent class

c) It is the process where the subclass tries to alter the way the parent class behaves

d) None of the above

Answer: C

Q4) How can you call an attribute called weight of an object called Lab?

a) >>> Lab.(weight)

   60

b) >>> Lab."weight"

   60

c) >>> Labweight

   60

d) >>> Lab.weight

   60

Answer: D

Chapter Nine: Dealing with the Unexpected

As in all kinds of programming, when working in Python, as a developer you are going to be facing both clients and users who won't exactly be clear on what they are looking for, and as such the program might get unexpected inputs. This chapter is all about teaching you how to deal with such problems.

When dealing such an unexpected situation, we say that we are facing an "Exception" – an event that was not supposed to happen.

For example, when you write a program where the program itself requires an input from the user, it might face a problem in the sense that the user enters something out of the program's range. In such a case, an error like this might occur:

```
TypeError: cannot concatenate 'str'
and
'int' objects
```

Another example that shows Python's error handling capability is as follows. This occurs when you have entered the wrong syntax – in this case, the absence of a colon.

```
>>> for x in range(5)
    File "<stdin>", line 1
      for x in range(5)
                      ^
SyntaxError: invalid syntax
```

Exception handling makes it really easy for a programmer or developer to debug the software and make sure that it runs as intended by using various statements.

Dealing with Problems Using Try/Except Statements

The first thing that comes to the mind of a programmer is to use the try or except block. It causes the "except" code to run only if the program faces an exception.

```
try:
        some code
except SomeException:
        exception-handling code
```

Python is intelligent enough to always keep track of what you are doing. Every time you call a function, Python immediately adds the call to a call stack which is stored as "traceback" that helps you to identify exactly when and where the error occurred, if any.

The following is an example of traceback.

```
### Three functions that call each
other
def a():
        b()
def b():
        c()
def c():
    1/0 # Attempt at division by
zero, will raise exception
### Run function a()
a()
```

When the above program is run, Python's traceback feature here lists the calls in the exact order they were received.

```
File "a.py", line 9, in <module>
        a()
File "a.py", line 3, in a
```

```
      b()
File "a.py", line 5, in b
      c()
File "a.py", line 7, in c
1/0                # Attempt at
division by
         zero, will raise exception
ZeroDivisionError: integer division
or
      modulo by zero
```

The methodology or internal working of Python here is as follows:

- Python first runs the try clause.
- If no exception is found, then Python eliminates the try block and restricts the program from running the except block.
- If an exception does occur, however, Python skips the rest of the try code and checks from the exception against the exception stated in the except statement. If Python finds a match, then Python goes on and executes the "except" clause.
- Otherwise, Python uses its built-in handler and prints an error message as shown earlier.

How to Handle Multiple Exceptions

By using the try/except codes, you will be able to process different kinds of exceptions as well. There are essentially two ways to do it:

- If you want to handle all of the caught exceptions in the same way, then what you will need to do is list all the exception classes inside a single except clause and pass the exception as a tuple.

```
except (RuntimeError,
TypeError, NameError):
```

- Alternatively, if you want to handle each exception in a different way, then you can use a multitude of except clauses. The multiple clauses are tested in a specific order. If the program finds a match with any of the clauses, then the rest are skipped.

```
except RuntimeError:
      some code
except TypeError:
      some different code
```

- Below is a simple example of a program that checks for the correct user input. If an error is found, then it goes for the try/except block and catches two different kinds of exceptions.

```
try:
    x = raw_input("Enter an integer:
")
    y = int(x)
    print "Your number was", y
except (TypeError, ValueError):
    print "That didn't
```

How to Process Exception Arguments

Exceptions are usually accompanied by a string that describes exactly what the problem is. For example:

```
try:
        x = int(x)
  except TypeError:
        raise TypeError("%r is not a
valid integer" % x)
```

However, if you want to further create a log of that exception, all you need to do is specify the name of the except statement that will hold the exception instance. In the following example, "detail" is used to keep the exception instance.

```
>>> try:
...     x = 1/0
... except ZeroDivisionError,
detail:
...     print "Oops,", detail
...
Oops, integer division or modulo by
zero
```

A Try/Except Block with an Else Clause

A try/except can be comprised of an else clause, which is only run after the try block has run successfully. Meaning, no exception is raised and no return or blocking statement is executed.

```
try:
    some code
except SomeException:
    exception-handling code
else:
    necessary code
```

Or more specifically, in a real example:

```
try:
      f = open('cheese_list')
      process(f) # This line is
pseudo-code
finally:
f.close()
```

The Try/Finally Statements

These statements are used whenever you are in need of a program that will always run as a part of the try block while handling the exceptions somewhere else in the program.

A typical try/finally block looks like this:

```
try:
      some code
finally:
      cleanup code
```

Chapter Nine: Study Questions

Q1) What is an Exception?

a) An event that is not some supposed to happen

b) An event without which the program can run

c) An event which the program is bound to face

d) An event which is normal, but will be run under certain conditions

Answer: A

Q2) Which one of the following is a valid Syntax for Exception handling

a) >>> for x in range(5)

    File "<stdin>", line 1

      for x in range(4)

         ^

    SyntaxError: invalid syntax

b) >>> for x in range(5)

    File "<stdin>", line 1

      for x in range(1)

         ^

    SyntaxError: invalid syntax

c) >>> for x in range(5)

    File "<stdin>", line 1

      for x in range(2)

SyntaxError: invalid syntax

d) >>> for x in range(5)

 File "<stdin>", line 1

  for x in range(5)

   ^

SyntaxError: invalid syntax

Answer: D

Q3) What happens when Python runs a clause and finds an exception?

a) It eliminates the try block and restricts the program from running the except block

b) It skips the rest of the try code and checks the exception against the exception stated in the except statement

c) It skips the rest of the try code and checks the exception against the exception stated in a specific formula

d) None of the above

Answer: B

Q4) Which of the following is a working example of try/except block with an else Clause

a) Try for:

 f = open('cheese_list')

 process(f) # This line is pseudo-code

```
    finally:
        f.close()
```
b) try if:
```
        f = open('cheese_list')
        process(f) # This line is pseudo-code
    finally:
        f.close()
```
c) try:
```
        f = open('cheese_list')
        process(f) # This line is pseudo-code
    finally:
        f.close
```
d) try:
```
        f = open('cheese_list')
        process(f) # This line is pseudo-code
    finally:
        f.close()
```
Answer: D

Chapter Ten: Some Common Mistakes and Useful Resources

We are all humans, right? Regardless of our skill level, we are still going to make teeny tiny mistakes here and there. And this is much more prominent in terms of new and budding programmers. In this chapter, we will be pointing out some of the most common mistakes that are made by freshly baked Python programmers as well as a small list of websites that will guide you to greatness in the long run.

The Common Mistakes

- **Misusing simple expressions by considering them as defaults for functional arguments**

Python has a very useful feature which allows you to specify a functional argument by giving it a default value. But this feature can sometimes cause some heavy confusion when the given value is mutable. To clear up the concept, let us look at the example below where we are defining a function:

```
>>>def foo(bar=[]): # bar is
optional and defaults to [] if not
```

```
Specified

...        bar.append("baz")     # but
this line could be problematic, as
we'll

See…

...        return bar
```

Here a very common mistake is to assume that the given optional argument will always be attached to the declared default expression every time the function is called without giving a value. In the given example above, one might think that when foo() is called without specifying the "bar," it will always return the value baz.

Let's have a look at what's really happening here.

```
>>>foo()

["baz"]

>>>foo()

["baz", "baz"]

>>>foo()

["baz", "baz", "baz"]
```

Did you notice what happened here? The foo() just kept appending the value of baz every single time it was called instead of creating a new list!

The reason for this is that the default value of a function argument is evaluated just once when the function is defined at the beginning.

A simple solution to this problem might be:

```
>>>def foo(bar=None):
...     if bar is None:      # or if not bar:
...         bar = []
...     bar.append("baz")
...     return bar
...
>>>foo()
["baz"]
>>>foo()
["baz"]
>>>foo()
```

```
["baz"]
```

- **Mishaps while using class variables**

Let's start this one by following through the given example.

```
>>> class A(object):
...         x = 1
...
>>> class B(A):
...         pass
...
>>> class C(A):
...         pass
...
>>> print A.x, B.x, C.x
1 1 1
```

Makes sense so far, yes?

But when you try to print them:

```
>>>B.x = 2

>>> print A.x, B.x, C.x

1 2 1
```

Alternatively:

```
>>>A.x = 3

>>> print A.x, B.x, C.x

3 2 3
```

See what is happening here? While you only changed the value of A.x, the value of C.x is automatically getting changed as well! This kind of problem occurs due to a lack of understanding of the way Python handles class variables. It is known as the Method Resolution Order (MRO). In the above example, since the value of x is absent in class C, the program goes above and looks for it in the base class. So, when printed, the value of C is taking the value from the class A. in other words, C.x is just a reference to A.x.

- **Not fully understanding the Python Scopes Regulations**

We have already discussed Python Scope at the beginning of the book, The Python Scope Regulation is primarily based on an LEGB rule, which stands for Local, Enclosing, Global, and Built In. But due to some very subtle indications in Python, programmers sometimes fail to realize how Python scopes actually work.

Consider the example below:

```
>>> x = 10
>>>deffoo():
...        x += 1
...        print x
...
>>>foo()
Traceback (most recent call last):
  File "<stdin>", line 1, in
<module>
  File "<stdin>", line 2, in foo
UnboundLocalError: local variable
'x' referenced before assignment
```

The error here occurs because you performed an assignment operation inside the given scope. If such an action is done, then Python automatically considers the variable to which something is assigned as local to the scope inside which the variable is, and causes it to neglect any similarly named variable outside that scope.

Thus many programmers are sometimes shocked when they receive the UnboundLocalError.

- **Attempting to modify a list while trying to iterate over it**

Just by taking a glance at the code below, the problem here should be pretty obvious.

```
>>> odd = lambda x : bool(x % 2)
>>> numbers = [n for n in range(10)]
>>> for i in range(len(numbers)):
...         if odd(numbers[i]):
...             del numbers[i]   # BAD:
Deleting item from a list while
iterating over it
...
```

```
Traceback (most recent call last):
    File "<stdin>", line 2, in
<module>
IndexError: list index out of range
```

Trying to delete an element from an iterating list or array is a problem that is well known to any amateur or experienced Python programmer. While the above example is pretty obvious, sometimes advanced developers might unintentionally face the same problem but via a much more complex code.

Luckily, however, Python is packed with a very useful number of programming paradigms which allows the developer to create much more streamlined and simplistic results. One of the paradigms that can be perfectly applied in this scenario to tackle the problem is known as the List Comprehension paradigm, which (as seen below) is a very potent solution to the problem at hand.

```
>>> odd = lambda x : bool(x % 2)
>>> numbers = [n for n in range(10)]
```

```
>>>numbers[:] = [n for n in numbers
if not odd(n)]  # ahh, the beauty of
it all

>>> numbers

[0, 2, 4, 6, 8]
```

- **Incorrect specification of parameters in exception blocks**

Assume that we have the code below:

```
>>> try:
...        l = ["a", "b"]
...        int(l[2])
... except ValueError, IndexError:
# To catch both exceptions, right?
...        pass
...
Traceback (most recent call last):
  File "<stdin>", line 3, in
<module>
IndexError: list index out of range
```

If you are not able to see the problem here, let me enlighten you. The except statement is not really designed to take lists of exception in the specified manner. Instead, from Python 2.x, the **except Exception, e** syntax is primarily used to bind an exception as an optional second specified secondary optional parameter. (In our case, it's e.) Therefore, in the given example, the **IndexError** exception is not being captured by except; rather, the exception itself falls down being named as **IndexError**.

The correct way to solve problems such as these is to specify the first parameter as being a tuple where all of the exceptions will be caught, as such:

```
>>> try:
...         l = ["a", "b"]
...         int(l[2])
... except (ValueError, IndexError) as e:
...         pass
...
>>>
```

A Bunch Of Resources

Below is a small list of websites from where you will be able to get most and possibly all solutions to your Python related problems.

- **The Big Mothership:** http://www.python.org

This website is widely regarded as being the Mothership of Python and it's for good reason! Python.org is a website that contains every single information documentation, download, FAQ, tutorial, and even a wiki related to Python Programming. There is a very nifty search engine which allows you to search everything and anything instantly with ease! And the best part is, the website is always constantly being updated – you won't be missing out on anything!

- **The Cheese Shop: A Whole World Of Modules**

The Cheese Shop, previously known as PyPI, is a website that holds a large collection of third-party designed Python modules. http://www.cheeseshop.python.org/
At the time of this writing, the website held a staggering number of packages: 1429. Most of the packages available on this website are free, requiring just a simple license verification scheme before allowing you to use them for commercial purposes.

- **The Great Reference Guide**

The page at http://www.wiki.python.org has a link to the Python Wiki. A wiki (for the newcomers out there) is a collection of highly detailed web pages that can be edited by anyone. Wikis generally use a lot of hyperlinks to send you jumping off from one page to the next in order to act as a vast information portal for you to pillage.

This website is a great place if you are looking for references to quickly get to know any concept that you might be missing from your Python knowledge.

Chapter Ten: Check Your Understanding

Q1) Why should you not consider simple expressions as defaults when dealing with functional arguments?

Q2) What are some common problems that might arise when dealing with class variables?

Q3) What problems might arise from not being able to understand the Python scope regulations?

Q4) What problems might arise by using incorrect parameters in Exception blocks

Conclusion

It has been a really long journey up until now hasn't it?

Let us take a moment here and thank you for bearing with us and reading this book up until the very end. We do hope you enjoyed reading this book as much as we enjoyed writing it for you.

With your current set of Python programming knowledge now and a little practice, you should be able to completely take the world of programming by storm with your creativity and intellectuality!

We have already mentioned a number of very useful websites which might act as your resource database. But regardless of from where you decide to gather up your amenities, what you should always keep in mind is "Practice makes a man perfect," and this is very much applicable in the world of Python. After completing this book, you should now keep on exploring as much as you can, keep practicing, and solve various problems around the web to expand your knowledge and create a strong foundation.

Have faith in yourself and eventually your effort will bear fruit, catapulting you into becoming one of the best Python Programmers in the world!

Contact Us

How can we make this book better for you?

Your suggestions, ideas, complaints will greatly help us. You can email us at Techshelve@gmail.com

Join Us -

You can receive offers and discounts on programming materials when you sign up for our email list: http://bit.ly/2cVwb18

www.ingramcontent.com/pod-product-compliance
Lightning Source LLC
Chambersburg PA
CBHW071200050326
40689CB00011B/2193